the Coupe

Celebrating
Craft Cocktails
and Vintage Collections

Brian Hart Hoffman

Foreword by Patrick Dunne

Cocktail and Food Photography
by Stephen DeVries

hm | books

the Coupe

CELEBRATING
CRAFT COCKTAILS
AND VINTAGE
COLLECTIONS

hm | books

PRESIDENT/CCO Brian Hart Hoffman
VICE PRESIDENT/EDITORIAL Cindy Smith Cooper
DIRECTOR OF EDITORIAL OPERATIONS Brooke Michael Bell
GROUP CREATIVE DIRECTOR Deanna Rippy Gardner

EDITORIAL

CREATIVE DIRECTOR/PHOTOGRAPHY Mac Jamieson
RECIPE EDITOR Fran Jensen
COPY EDITOR Whitney Durrwachter
COCKTAIL AND FOOD PHOTOGRAPHY Stephen DeVries
STYLISTS Lucy Herndon, Mary Beth Jones
FOOD STYLISTS Vanessa Rocchio, Anita Simpson Spain, Loren Wood
SENIOR DIGITAL IMAGING SPECIALIST Delisa McDaniel
DIGITAL IMAGING SPECIALIST Clark Densmore

hm
hoffmanmedia

CHAIRMAN OF THE BOARD/CEO Phyllis Hoffman DePiano
PRESIDENT/COO Eric W. Hoffman
PRESIDENT/CCO Brian Hart Hoffman
EXECUTIVE VICE PRESIDENT/CFO Mary P. Cummings
EXECUTIVE VICE PRESIDENT/OPERATIONS & MANUFACTURING
Greg Baugh
VICE PRESIDENT/DIGITAL MEDIA Jon Adamson
VICE PRESIDENT/EDITORIAL Cindy Smith Cooper
VICE PRESIDENT/INTEGRATED MARKETING SOLUTIONS
Ray Reed
VICE PRESIDENT/ADMINISTRATION Lynn Lee Terry

Hoffman Media
1900 International Park Drive, Suite 50
Birmingham, Alabama 35243
hoffmanmedia.com

ISBN: 978-1-940772-24-0
Printed in China

*To coupe lovers everywhere:
May you entertain at home in
style with these craft cocktails*

CONTENTS

Foreword

It is rare for any 10 year old to regard his parents as flawless, but that moment in the late 1950s is still distinct when, peering over some awful lemonade spruced up with grenadine, I observed my mother comfortably settled against the old leather banquette in the bar of the Gran Hotel Ancira, her cream silk skirt printed by Madame Trigère with large cabbage-colored flowers fully spread out over the cushioned seat. She lifted her Manhattan for a perfect clink with my father's Whiskey Sour to celebrate the beginning of their getaway to Mexico. It seemed he was only happy when he was south of the border, and his tan face relaxed above his starched linen suit. I thought them both fabulous and could not wait to be an adult and clink a real drink.

For nearly a century, no single image has been more iconic of ultrachic than a well-tailored arm and manicured fingers wrapped around the stem of a frosty cocktail coupe. Even a wine glass awash with some deep red rare vintage does not convey quite the instant message of sophistication. No doubt some of this is rooted in the breakout decades following the First World War, when a new freedom and new fun was associated with jazz, wild dancing, and creative cocktails. The saxophone and the cocktail glass became enduring emblems of the high life.

Gorgeous and conniving film stars reinforced this perception for decades and created a juggernaut of imitation. Women (and not just "flappers") asserted the right to bob their hair, speak their minds, vote, and drink in public. It is an irony that once in possession of the ballot, women voted *en bloc* for Prohibition. Nevertheless, American women were the first to demand a special costume for this new ritual of cocktails, and French couturiers, greedy for trans-Atlantic clientele, obliged with a hybrid frock that was neither daywear nor evening gown but somewhere in between, appropriate for *l'heure de cocktail*. In the 1940s, Christian Dior was the first house to actually name a garment a "cocktail dress," but by that time it was already *de rigueur* for all well-heeled ladies.

...THE CRAZE FOR STRAINING MARTINIS, MANHATTANS, SIDECARS, BRANDY ALEXANDERS, AND A PLETHORA OF OTHER DRINKS INTO COUPES WAS DEFINITELY A CONCEIT OF THE EARLY 20TH CENTURY.

Despite being linked in the popular mind to the Roaring 20s, "the cocktail" is considerably older and may be one of our country's original contributions to culinary history. Several Victorian lexicographers tried to trace the term back to the American Revolution; whether that is far-fetched or not, the expression had certainly found its way into usage by the mid-19th century. Like all new religious cults, there was no precise agreement on what constituted orthodoxy. The definition of a cocktail seemed to hinge on a distinction between the "highball," which was spirits mixed with water or some other liquid, and the more complex "cocktail," which had at least three ingredients (preferably two of which were alcoholic). In addition to liquor, cocktails invariably contained bitters and often sweetener.

One of the earliest serious American bar guides I know of was published in 1862 by Jerry Thomas, and among hundreds of recipes for punches, toddies, slings, "sangarees," and cordials, there is a section on cocktails. Thomas, writing on the eve of the Civil War, observes that the cocktail "is a modern invention and is generally used on fishing and other sporting parties, although some 'patients' insist that it is good in the morning as a tonic." Included in his lists is a protean recipe for that quintessential refreshment, the Old Fashioned, which he calls simply a "Whiskey Cocktail." A celebrity in his own time, Thomas presided over renowned bars at the Metropolitan Hotel in New York City, St. Louis, and also New Orleans, where he owned an establishment. Along with San Francisco, these eventually would become the epicenters of cocktail ferment.

The bar and cocktail craze blazed through the early 20th century, only to crash a decade before the stock market with the onset of Prohibition. Those 13 mad years of spirituous suppression meant that a number of eminent barmen who had developed great and original recipes retired, changed professions, or emigrated to friendlier jurisdictions as famous barrooms across the country were forced to close. In the shuffle, many of their signature drinks were lost, as they existed only in oral tradition and, like jazz, were frequently improvisational. By default, Paris and London began to flourish as important centers carrying on the cocktail legacy. To convince patrons of competence, drinks there often bore American names or allusions, and the first American-trained mixologist "called to the bar" in a London hotel made his debut in the summer of 1920. Some mavericks in the States chose to flaunt the law, or serve in shadowy venues like private yachts and pleasure boats.

In a funny way, Prohibition ultimately promoted rather than stunted the development of cocktail culture. Experiences with "bathtub gin" and other rotgut distillations led to experiments with extreme flavorings to cover unpleasant tastes, which meant Americans developed a penchant for crude and often sweet combinations that endured even after Repeal. The Volstead Act had hardly cooled in its constitutional grave when the foundational *The Old Waldorf-Astoria Bar Book* was "reprinted." It was in fact a compilation of more than 500 recipes for cocktails served at New York's most famous bar before "the great drought," as Prohibition was sometimes tagged.

It is curious that early manuals for cocktails, whether the classic bartenders' guides composed between 1890 and 1919 or later savvy compendiums like Charles Baker's *The Gentleman's Companion*, offer little guidance as to what type of glass to use. There is much emphasis on ingredients, preparations, shakings, and chilling but nothing on the appropriate stemware. It was assumed that all this was understood as a matter of common sense. Certainly highballs called for a tall glass or tumbler, and flutes were still fashionable with old-timers for Champagne, but the craze for straining Martinis, Manhattans, Sidecars, Brandy Alexanders, and a plethora of other drinks into coupes was definitely a conceit of the early 20th century. How exactly it happened is still uncertain.

THE MYTHICAL LINEAGE CLAIMING THE ORIGINAL COUPE WAS FORMED FROM A MOLD OF MARIE ANTOINETTE'S BOSOM, WHILE CHARMING, IS PROBABLY SCURRILOUS.

The coupe as a type of drinking vessel has been around for a long time. Its ancient ancestor was certainly the chalice, which was no more than a cup on a stylized foot. The end of the Renaissance Venice, synthesizer of all oriental refinements for Europe, produced the first fine glass tableware. The Musée du Verre in Liège, along with countless collections in Europe and America, has a number of 16th-century examples of broad-mouthed, shallow bowls set on extravagant twisted stems. These improbable glasses would make any fancy contemporary bartender's mouth water.

The mythical lineage claiming the original coupe was formed from a mold of Marie Antoinette's bosom, while charming, is probably scurrilous. Political rhetoric was no kinder then than it is now, and any foul thing populist pamphleteers could fabricate to demean the French royal circle found its way into print. Alas later serious English writers on glass, often unconscious Francophobes, repeated the story. Its one link to any historical reality lay in the fact that Louis XVI ordered, as a surprise gift for his queen, an exquisite biscuit porcelain service from Sèvres. The design was based on the ancient Greek Mastos cup, which was in the form of a female breast on a tripod. Production was interrupted by the Revolution so only some pieces were delivered, and far from being used to swill potent potables, these vessels were actually intended for drinking milk and taking desserts in the Queen's lovely pale gray and white laiterie at the Château de Rambouillet.

In fact, there are clear examples of the coupe form in household inventories well before Marie Antoinette's day, some as early as 1760. Whether these glasses were used to drink from or to serve up desserts is another question altogether. Candied fruits and syllabubs, as well as other custard-type desserts, were much in vogue in the 18th century and part of the classic privileged menu. It is said the epicurean Marquis Charles de Saint-Evrémond, exiled by Louis Quatorze, taught the English to love Champagne

and drink it stylishly from flutes. This method of taking the new drink stayed in vogue for nearly two centuries. It seems likely that a creative hostess sometime in the mid-19th century, bored with old routines and determined to make a fashion statement, took the dessert coupe and filled it with Champagne. By the Belle Époque, the coupe was ubiquitous. Suddenly ladies partaking of the beverage preferred to have fewer bubbles, the long stem prevented the bowl from warming, and besides, it seemed ever so much more elegant.

Short was the hopscotch for this top-heavy bowl from dessert to effervescence to cocktails. And the propinquity of cocktails to desserts is telling. The humble highball did not rely on sugar, whereas the complex, ever amorphous cocktail often relied on ingredients that added aromatics and sweeteners to the spirits. This was like a genie let out of its bottle, challenging the imagination and teasing the palate, and it was a genie who found in the coupe a comfortable home to curl.

The cocktail craze has ebbed and flowed in the ensuing years. Costumes, customs, and some of the rituals may have changed, but now in our own "new" century, we have seen a true revival of the elegantly crafted cocktail, as well as the celebrity bartender. While *The Old Waldorf-Astoria Bar Book* has ideas aplenty to quench the most exigent thirst, contemporary mixologists have brought new creativity to the pursuit, with inventive infusions and avant-garde techniques that might have awed even the old guard barmen. The virtuoso recipes found in this book are testimony that the genie is still doing his work at the bar. Through all of these caprices of style and taste, the haughty coupe has held its primacy of place.

— PATRICK DUNNE, AUTHOR OF *THE EPICUREAN COLLECTOR* AND PROPRIETOR OF LUCULLUS IN NEW ORLEANS, LOUISIANA, WHICH BOASTS AN INTERNATIONAL CLIENTELE BECAUSE OF ITS UNIQUE EMPHASIS ON ANTIQUES, ART, AND OBJECTS WITH A CULINARY CONNECTION

The Art OF

A BEAUTIFUL BAR SHOULD
REFLECT YOUR PERSONALITY AND
HAVE LAYERS OF STYLE, VARYING
HEIGHTS AND TEXTURES, AND
OBJECTS OF INTEREST BESIDES
YOUR FAVORITE COUPE GLASSES

THE Home Bar

FAVORITE ACCESSORIES FOR THE ULTIMATE BAR CART STYLE

★ Spirits in a variety of
  shapes and colors
  and small bottles such
  as bitters

★ Decanters

★ Vintage Champagne or
  ice buckets (great for
  flowers or wine corks)

★ Bar and cocktail books

★ An assortment of
  cocktail napkins (They
  don't have to be a
  perfect set. Mix and
  match your favorite
  monograms.)

★ Bar tools (new and
  antique such as horn-
  handled bottle openers
  and sterling jiggers)

★ Drink stirrers and olive
  spoons

★ Wooden muddler

★ Cocktail shakers

★ Trays for corralling and
  layering

★ Artwork

★ Bowls for cocktail nuts
  and citrus garnishes

Tips for Collecting Coupes

From vintage to new, my advice for collecting coupes: Buy what you love. As you build your collection, purchase a variety of sizes and silhouettes, from statuesque stems to chunky cut glass, and don't feel confined to using a matching set when entertaining. Show off your coupes, and serve cocktails in an assortment of styles. Larger coupes are great for serving elegant desserts that are easy to prepare ahead. (See recipes on page 110.)

Coupes can be purchased at antiques stores, junk shops, flea markets, online auctions, and traditional retailers. If you're searching for vintage coupes, there's no rule of thumb to what you should pay. Many great coupes can be scored for a few dollars or less. Set a maximum price for what you want to pay, and have fun collecting. When buying vintage, be sure to carefully inspect each coupe for chips and cracks, and don't let a little dust or dirt scare you.

If you're looking to focus your collection, use a thread such as gold and silver rims, etched glass, or cut glass. Have fun coupin', and enjoy the coupe life.

Sparkling Cocktails

THE CLASSIC CHAMPAGNE
COCKTAIL GETS A
MODERN UPDATE

Sparkling Cocktails

PEPPINO
DI CAPRI

Masseria, Washington, DC

Makes 1 serving

1   ounce high-quality vodka
1   tablespoon seasonal sorbet
Prosecco

1. Pour vodka into a coupe glass. Create a quenelle (egg-shaped scoop) of sorbet, and drop into glass. (The traditional flavor is lemon, but any seasonal flavor works well, like raspberry or blood orange.) Top with Prosecco. If preferred, serve with a demitasse spoon.

Masseria

This refreshing cocktail is Masseria's innovative version of a Sgroppino, a cocktail originating in Venice, Italy, that consists of lemon sorbet, vodka, and Prosecco.

Birds & Bubbles

Designed by bartender John Evans, the Dawg Gone't at Birds & Bubbles features notes of brûléed plums elevated through the crisp brioche character of Gonet-Médeville's Brut Champagne.

Dawg Gone't

Birds & Bubbles, New York, New York

Makes 1 serving

1   ounce Greenhook Ginsmiths Beach Plum Gin
     Liqueur
¾   ounce Napoleon Amontillado Sherry
¾   ounce Simple Syrup (recipe on page 133)
½   ounce fresh lemon juice
1   large egg white
Gonet-Médeville 1er Cru Tradition Brut
     Champagne
Garnish: expressed orange peel

1. In a cocktail shaker, add gin liqueur, sherry,
Simple Syrup, and lemon juice. Shake to combine.
Add egg white and ice, and shake until cold. Double
strain into a coupe glass, and top with Champagne.
Garnish with expressed orange peel, if desired.

Mazoma

Burlock Coast, The Ritz-Carlton, Fort Lauderdale, Florida

Makes 1 serving

½   ounce Plantation 3 Stars Silver Rum
½   ounce D'Aristi Xtabentún*
SYLTBAR Premium Prosecco
Garnish: shoot of sugarcane, julienned

1. Pour rum and Xtabentún into a chilled coupe glass; gently swirl. Top with Prosecco, and garnish with julienned sugarcane, if desired.

*Yucatán regional anise, distilled honey, and rum liqueur.

Burlock Coast

Inspired by Ernest Hemingway's Death in the Afternoon cocktail, this cocktail's name loosely translates to "he rages over drink" in the Nahuatl language. With rum, Xtabentún, and bubbles, this Burlock Coast cocktail created by James Camp is sure to light a fire in the belly of the imbiber.

Acadiana

Louisianan Creole culture is heavily influenced by the French, and that same culture defines Acadiana's version of this popular cocktail. Scott Clime, Wine & Beverage Director, uses Hennessy Cognac—like the French do—in place of the gin.

FRENCH 75

Acadiana, Washington, DC

Makes 1 serving

1 ounce Hennessy V.S
¾ ounce Simple Syrup (recipe on page 133)
½ ounce fresh lemon juice
3 ounces sparkling wine
Garnish: lemon twist

1. In a cocktail shaker filled with ice, add Hennessy, Simple Syrup, and lemon juice. Shake to combine, and strain into a coupe glass. Top with sparkling wine. Garnish with a lemon twist, if desired.

STRAWBERRY SPARKLER

Brennan's Restaurant, New Orleans, Louisiana

Makes 1 serving

2   ounces cold Strawberry Basil Syrup (recipe follows)
3 to 4 ounces Champagne or sparkling wine
Garnish: fresh basil leaf

1. Place cold Strawberry Basil Syrup in a coupe glass. Add Champagne or sparkling wine to fill. Garnish with basil, if desired.

STRAWBERRY BASIL SYRUP

1   pint Louisiana strawberries, chopped into quarters
¼   cup sugar
1   cup very hot water
½   cup fresh basil leaves

1. Muddle strawberries with sugar to break berries down until sugar is saturated with juice. Add 1 cup water and basil, and let mixture steep for 20 minutes. Stir and double strain until juice is free of seeds. Refrigerate mixture for up to 1 week.

Brennan's Restaurant

Brennan's, the iconic establishment in New Orleans's French Quarter, offers this seasonal sparkler. This pink beauty is the most popular drink during the renowned "Bubbles at Brennan's" happy hour at Roost Bar.

Vodka

SOPHISTICATED AND SLEEK, THESE VODKA
COCKTAILS ARE FAR FROM BORING

THE COUPE | CHAPTER TWO

NASHVILLE '75

The Farm House, Nashville, Tennessee

Makes 1 serving

1½   ounces Pickers Blood Orange Vodka
1   ounce Nash '75 Syrup (recipe follows)
2   dashes fresh lemon juice
Sparkling wine
Garnish: fresh mint sprig

1. In a cocktail shaker filled with ice, add vodka, Nash '75 Syrup, and lemon juice. Shake to combine. Strain into a coupe glass, and top with sparkling wine. Garnish with mint, if desired.

NASH '75 SYRUP

Muddle a fresh mint sprig and a coin-size slice of fresh ginger with 1 ounce Simple Syrup (recipe on page 133).

The Farm House

The classic Champagne cocktail at The Farm House is made a little bit country and all Nashville by General Manager and Beverage Director Larry Sinclair. The wonderful flavor of SPEAKeasy Spirits' Pickers Blood Orange Vodka is highlighted and not covered up.

Easy Bistro & Bar

The Mountain Rose at Easy Bistro & Bar is lightly sweet and floral with a hint of hoppiness from the Hophead Vodka. Designed by Bar Manager Alex Jump, it's a cocktail that is lower in alcohol, so it's a perfect apéritif for the beginning of a meal.

MOUNTAIN ROSE

Easy Bistro & Bar, Chattanooga, Tennessee

Makes 1 serving

1   ounce Tempus Fugit Crème de Noyaux
½   ounce Hophead Vodka
¼   ounce fresh lime juice
¼   ounce fresh grapefruit juice
Sparkling wine
Garnish: fresh lavender or local edible flower

1. In a cocktail shaker filled with ice, add Tempus Fugit Crème de Noyaux, vodka, lime juice, and grapefruit juice. Shake to combine, and double strain into a coupe glass. Top with sparkling wine, and garnish with lavender or local flower, if desired.

Vodka

WITHIN TEMPTATION

The Cocktail Club, Charleston, South Carolina

Makes 1 serving

1¾   ounces Dixie Black Pepper Vodka
½   ounce blanc vermouth
¼   ounce Dixie Southern Vodka
¼   ounce blue cheese tincture
1   dash celery bitters
1   dash lemon bitters
Garnish: chilled blue cheese wedge, lemon twist

1. In a mixing glass filled with ice, stir together Dixie Black Pepper Vodka, vermouth, Dixie Southern Vodka, blue cheese tincture, and bitters. Strain into a coupe glass, and garnish with blue cheese and a lemon twist, if desired.

The Cocktail Club

Looking for a way to incorporate blue cheese flavor
into drinks without having to continuously stuff olives,
Jeremiah Schenzel at Charleston's The Cocktail Club
created the Within Temptation. After many failed
attempts, he found blue cheese tincture was the key and
a perfect combination with Dixie Black Pepper Vodka.

From the Author

For Brian Hart Hoffman and Brooke Bell, summer in the South means one thing: It's time for an Alabama Summer. This drink combines Brian's love for a watermelon margarita with Brooke's passion for Tito's Handmade Vodka. Campari's bitterness balances the sweet watermelon juice, and a splash of sparkling water adds a finishing touch.

ALABAMA
SUMMER

Makes 1 serving

3   ounces fresh watermelon juice
1½   ounces Tito's Handmade Vodka
½ to ¾ ounce Campari
½   ounce fresh lime juice
1 to 2 ounces chilled sparkling water
Garnish: sliced watermelon

1. In a cocktail shaker filled with ice, add
watermelon juice, vodka, Campari, and lime juice.
Shake to combine, and strain into a coupe glass. Top
with sparkling water, and garnish with a watermelon
slice, if desired.

Vodka

SOMETIMES, ALWAYS, NEVER

Chesa, Portland, Oregon

Makes 1 serving

2   ounces lemongrass-infused vodka*
½   ounce manzanilla sherry
½   ounce dry Spanish vermouth
2 to 3 drops saline solution (1 part salt to 10 parts
      water)
Garnish: preserved lemon slice

1. In a mixing glass filled with ice, add vodka, sherry, vermouth, and saline solution. Stir to combine, and strain into a coupe glass. Garnish with preserved lemon slice, if desired.

*Bar Manager Tony Gurdian does a rapid infusion on the lemongrass with an iSi gourmet whip, but you can simply macerate the lemongrass in the vodka.

Chesa

A play on the classic drink called the Tuxedo, the "Sometimes, Always, Never" at Chesa refers to the rule to follow for which buttons to fasten on a man's sports coat. Bar Manager Tony Gurdian uses lemongrass-infused vodka to match up with manzanilla sherry, which provides a maritime quality, and dry vermouth helps further aromatize.

Gin

ALWAYS-REFRESHING GIN
MEETS THE COUPE WITH
THESE CRAFT COCKTAILS

Arugula Martini

Marcel's, Washington, DC

Makes 2 servings

1	handful fresh arugula
2	ounces Hendrick's Gin
1	ounce fresh lime juice
¾	ounce St. Germain
½	ounce agave nectar

Garnish: arugula leaves, cracked pepper

1. In a cocktail shaker, add arugula, gin, lime juice, St. Germain, and agave nectar. Shake to combine. Using a wooden spoon, mash until arugula is wilted. Add ice, and shake briefly. Strain into 2 coupe glasses, and garnish each with an arugula leaf and cracked pepper, if desired.

Marcel's

At Marcel's, the cold-pressed juice craze
has "spilled over" into the realms of fanciful
cocktails thanks to this innovative libation,
prepared by combining fresh arugula leaves
with agave nectar. Fresh lime juice is then
splashed in for a tart, citric kick.

Edmund's Oast

Jayce McConnell's The Day After
the Day of the Dead cocktail at
Edmund's Oast captures the essence
of the Corpse Reviver #2. By
substituting some ingredients, the
drink has an earthy, spicy kick while
preserving its vibrant citrus zip.

The Day After The Day of The Dead

Edmund's Oast, Charleston, South Carolina

Makes 1 serving

¾ ounce St. George Dry Rye Reposado Gin
¾ ounce Lillet Blanc
¾ ounce Chile-Infused Pierre Ferrand Dry Curaçao (recipe follows)
¾ ounce fresh lemon juice
1 eyedropper Bittermens Hellfire Habanero Shrub
Garnish: grapefruit peel

1. In a cocktail shaker filled with ice, add gin, Lillet Blanc, Chile-Infused Pierre Ferrand Dry Curaçao, lemon juice, and shrub. Shake to combine. Double strain into a coupe glass, and garnish with a grapefruit peel, if desired.

Chile-Infused Pierre Ferrand Dry Curaçao

1 tablespoon crushed red pepper
1 (750-ml) bottle Pierre Ferrand Dry Curaçao

1. Pour red pepper into curaçao bottle. Cover and infuse for 15 minutes, shaking occasionally. Strain through a fine-mesh sieve, discarding solids.

GARNET

Bottega, Birmingham, Alabama

Makes 1 serving

1½ ounces Plymouth Gin
1 ounce fresh pomegranate juice
½ ounce Combier L'Original
Foggy Ridge Serious Cider
Garnish: lemon peel

1. In a cocktail shaker filled with ice, add gin, pomegranate juice, and Combier L'Original. Shake to combine. Muddle, and strain into a chilled coupe glass. Top with Foggy Ridge Serious Cider, and garnish with a lemon peel, if desired.

Bottega

It is said that the garnet gemstone was named for the color of
pomegranates, and this cocktail, crafted by Bottega Beverage
Director Matt Gilpin, is so named to reflect its essence.

Bacon Bros. Public House

The Kollar was the last drink that longtime bartender Ryan Kollar worked on before he was killed in a car accident in May 2015. Although the cocktail is seasonal, Beverage Director Gabriel Ayers at Bacon Bros. Public House leaves it on the menu year-round as a memorial to Ryan.

The Kollar

Bacon Bros. Public House, Greenville, South Carolina

Makes 1 serving

1   ounce Pineapple Sage-Infused Gin (recipe
     follows)
¾   ounce Green Chartreuse
½   ounce fresh lemon juice
½   ounce egg white
½   ounce Simple Syrup (recipe on page 133)
1   dash Angostura Bitters
Garnish: fresh pineapple sage

1. In a cocktail shaker, add Pineapple Sage-Infused
Gin, Green Chartreuse, lemon juice, egg white,
Simple Syrup, and bitters. Shake to combine, and
strain into a chilled coupe glass. Garnish with sage
and additional bitters, if desired.

Pineapple Sage-Infused Gin
Add 1 cup pineapple sage leaves and ½ cup lemon
balm leaves to ½ gallon gin. Let stand for 2 weeks to
infuse, and strain before using.

"You're Turning Violet, Violet"

PassionFish, Bethesda, Maryland

Makes 1 serving

1½ ounces Lavender-Infused Edinburgh Gin
   (recipe follows)
¾ ounce Dolin Dry Vermouth
¾ ounce Cointreau
Garnish: orange twist

1. In a cocktail shaker filled with ice, add Lavender-Infused Edinburgh Gin, vermouth, and Cointreau. Shake to combine, and strain into a coupe glass. Garnish with an orange twist, if desired.

Lavender-Infused Edinburgh Gin

In a medium saucepan, heat 2 teaspoons dried lavender over low heat. Add 2 cups gin, and bring to a boil. Remove from heat, and let cool. Add remainder of bottle of gin, strain through a piece of cheesecloth, and rebottle.

PassionFish

Your favorite stubborn character from *Willy Wonka and the Chocolate Factory* is immortalized in this PassionFish cocktail, created by Scott Clime, Wine & Beverage Director, made from mixing Lavender-Infused Edinburgh Gin with Cointreau and Dolin Dry Vermouth.

Russell House Tavern

Inspired by the classic cocktail of both Peru and Chile, the Pisco Sour, this Russell House Tavern drink uses Aperol as a sweetener and Regans' Orange Bitters No. 6 to give further punch and complexity.

THE SPACE BETWEEN THE STARS

Russell House Tavern, Cambridge, Massachusetts

Makes 1 serving

1	ounce Aperol
½	ounce Pisco Portón La Caravedo
½	ounce Regans' Orange Bitters No. 6
¼	ounce fresh lemon juice
¼	ounce fresh lime juice
1	large egg white

1. In a cocktail shaker, add all ingredients. Shake to combine. Add ice, and shake until cold. Strain into a coupe glass.

Texas Sling

Jack Allen's Kitchen, Austin, Texas

Makes 1 serving

3	ounces pineapple juice
1½	ounces Austin Reserve gin
½	ounce Paula's Texas Orange
½	ounce Cherry Heering
½	ounce Housemade Grenadine (recipe follows)
½	ounce fresh lime juice
1	dash Angostura Bitters

Garnish: orange twist, Luxardo or maraschino cherry

1. In a cocktail shaker filled with ice, add pineapple juice, gin, Paula's Texas Orange, Cherry Heering, Housemade Grenadine, lime juice, and bitters. Shake to combine, and strain into a coupe glass. Garnish with an orange twist and a cherry, if desired.

Housemade Grenadine

In a 4-quart saucepan, add 2 bottles pomegranate juice (such as POM Wonderful). Bring to a slight boil, and reduce heat. Add 3 cups sugar, and stir until dissolved. Add 2 ounces pomegranate molasses and 1 teaspoon orange blossom water. Remove from heat, and let cool. Grenadine can be kept in refrigerator for up to 3 weeks. Add 1 ounce vodka to preserve longer, if needed.

Jack Allen's Kitchen

A play on the traditional Singapore Sling, this gin cocktail, developed by Jack Allen's Kitchen Bar Manager David Toby, pairs traditional ingredients and local Texas spirits to create a refreshing daytime drink with bright fruit notes.

Rum

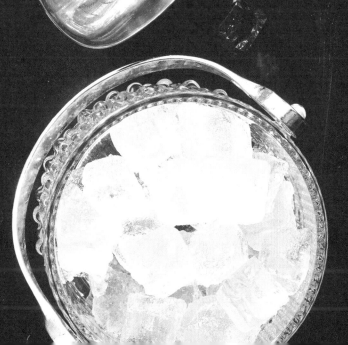

FROM MILK PUNCH TO
A TAKE ON THE CLASSIC
DAIQUIRI, RUM SHINES
IN A COUPE

From the Author

Bermuda's iconic Rum Swizzle
gets an update with fresh
blood orange juice.

BERMUDIAN RUM SWIZZLE

Makes 1 serving

2	ounces pineapple juice
2	ounces fresh blood orange juice
1½	ounces Gosling's Black Seal Rum
½	ounce fresh lemon juice
½	ounce fresh lime juice
½	ounce grenadine
1	dash blood orange bitters

Garnish: sliced blood orange

1. In a cocktail shaker filled with ice, add pineapple juice, orange juice, rum, lemon juice, lime juice, grenadine, and bitters. Shake to combine, and strain into a coupe glass. Garnish with a blood orange slice, if desired.

Rum

Tituba

Isla, Austin, Texas

Makes 1 serving

1½   ounces Nicaraguan rum
1½   ounces coconut cream
½   ounce fresh lime juice
1   jalapeño, muddled
Garnish: fresh basil leaf

1. In a cocktail shaker filled with ice, add rum, coconut cream, lime juice, and muddled jalapeño. Shake to combine, and strain into a coupe glass filled with crushed ice. Garnish with basil, if desired.

Isla

Blending the persistence of coconut, the bright bite of jalapeño, and the bold mellow taste of Nicaraguan rum, this cocktail, crafted by Isla's Miguel Lopez, is named after the first woman burned in the Salem Witch Trials. That's why it has a little bit of heat under it.

The Wayland

AFROHEAD Rum's use of bourbon barrels brings forth a wonderful mixture of honey, vanilla, and oak accents. The Wayland's Mackenzie Gleason blends the rum with Sarsaparilla Root Syrup to create the Sugarfoot, named in reference to an old western TV show in which the main character, Tom Brewster, would order a "sarsaparilla" soda.

SUGARFOOT

The Wayland, New York, New York

Makes 1 serving

2	ounces AFROHEAD Rum Briland 07
1	ounce Sarsaparilla Root Syrup (recipe follows)
½	ounce fresh lemon juice
½	ounce fresh lime juice
1	dash Angostura Bitters
1	dash black walnut bitters
1	large egg white

Garnish: Angostura Bitters

1. In a cocktail shaker, add rum, Sarsaparilla Root Syrup, lemon juice, lime juice, bitters, and egg white. Shake to combine. Add ice, and shake until cold. Strain into a coupe glass, and garnish with bitters, if desired.

SARSAPARILLA ROOT SYRUP
Makes 3 cups

2	cups sarsaparilla root
1	cup water
2	cups Simple Syrup (recipe on page 133)

1. In a medium saucepan, bring sarsaparilla root and 1 cup water to a boil. Let steep for 30 minutes. Strain mixture, discarding root, and add Simple Syrup. Let cool. (Place in an ice bath to speed up the cooling process.) — *Mackenzie Gleason and Reuben Perez*

CARIBBEAN MILK PUNCH

Brennan's Restaurant, New Orleans, Louisiana

Makes 1 serving

1	ounce Smith & Cross or Mount Gay Black Barrel Rum
½	ounce Maker's Mark or Buffalo Trace Bourbon
1	ounce Vanilla Syrup (recipe on page 133)
1	ounce heavy whipping cream

Garnish: hand-shaved nutmeg

1. In a cocktail shaker filled with ice, add rum, bourbon, Vanilla Syrup, and cream. Shake to combine, and strain into a coupe glass. Garnish with nutmeg, if desired.

Brennan's Restaurant

Milk Punch has been a classic cocktail at Brennan's, a New Orleans icon, for over 70 years, and with its recent relaunch, the establishment has put a new spin on this white sensation with their Caribbean Milk Punch. Vanilla bean-infused simple syrup and a hand-grated nutmeg garnish add an aromatic essence to this creamy Caribbean rum cocktail.

Aviary

"The first of many" cocktails Bar Manager
Justin Garcidiaz developed for Aviary, this
drink is a take on the classic daiquiri. It includes
the addition of allspice dram, for a hint of
spice, and celery bitters, to impart a savory
quality that balances out the acid of the lime.

THE FIRST OF MANY

Aviary, Portland, Oregon

Makes 1 serving

1½   ounces Pyrat XO Reserve Rum
1   ounce fresh lime juice
½   ounce Simple Syrup (recipe on page 133)
¼   ounce allspice dram
2   dashes Scrappy's Celery Bitters
Garnish: lime slice

1. In a cocktail shaker filled with ice, add rum, lime juice, Simple Syrup, allspice dram, and bitters. Shake to combine, and strain into a coupe glass. Garnish with a lime slice, if desired.

Tequila

SHAKEN WITH CITRUS AND
HINTS OF SPICE—TEQUILA
BELONGS IN A COUPE

LAVAGAVE

Beaker & Gray, Miami, Florida

Makes 1 serving

1   ounce Don Julio Blanco Tequila
¾   ounce lavender agave
½   ounce Fidencio Clásico Joven Mezcal
½   ounce fresh grapefruit juice
½   ounce fresh lime juice
3   dashes Bittercube Cherry Bark Vanilla Bitters
1   large egg white
Garnish: fresh lavender

1. In a cocktail shaker, add tequila, lavender agave, mezcal, grapefruit juice, lime juice, bitters, and egg white. Shake to combine. Add ice, and shake until cold. Strain into a coupe glass, and garnish with lavender, if desired.

Beaker & Gray

The Lavagave, created by Ben Potts, is a refreshing
combination of bright tequila, smoky and earthy mezcal,
and light and delicate lavender. A harmonious balance is
created between two seemingly different ingredients—
lavender and agave—in this Beaker & Gray cocktail.

Porchlight

Inspired by the flashy, colorful, head-turning street cocktails of New Orleans, Nicholas Bennett's Gun Metal Blue may look super sweet, but the Blue Curaçao is balanced out by smoky flavors and a bitterness that gives this Porchlight cocktail a backbone.

Gun Metal Blue

Porchlight, New York, New York

Makes 1 serving

1½   ounces Vida Mezcal
¾   ounce fresh lime juice
½   ounce Blue Curaçao
¼   ounce peach brandy
¼   ounce Bitter Cinnamon Simple Syrup (recipe
      follows)
Garnish: orange coin

1. In a cocktail shaker filled with ice, add mezcal, lime juice, Blue Curaçao, brandy, and Bitter Cinnamon Simple Syrup. Shake to combine, and strain into a coupe glass. Garnish with an orange coin, if desired.

Bitter Cinnamon Simple Syrup

4   sticks cinnamon
4   cups sugar
2   cups water
2   ounces gentian root

1. Break apart cinnamon, and place in a saucepan. Heat over low heat until cinnamon becomes aromatic. Add sugar, 2 cups water, and gentian root to pan, and heat until sugar has dissolved and mixture is at a low simmer. Remove from heat, and let cool. Strain and refrigerate.

PRIMO!

Odd Duck, Austin, Texas

Makes 1 serving

2	ounces Wahaka Mezcal
¾	ounce fresh lemon juice
¾	ounce Simple Syrup (recipe on page 133)
¾	ounce Habañero Brine (recipe follows)

Fresh cilantro leaves
Garnish: fresh cilantro leaves

1. In a cocktail shaker filled with ice, add mezcal, lemon juice, Simple Syrup, Habañero Brine, and cilantro. Shake to combine, and double strain into a coupe glass. Garnish with cilantro, if desired.

HABAÑERO BRINE

Make a salt brine, and rest habañeros for 2 weeks in solution. Make sure to use proper canning methods to ward off any unwanted friends. After fermented in the brine, strain out peppers, and cut the brine with filtered water (1 part brine, 3 parts filtered water).

Odd Duck

Simple in its nature but packing a serious punch, the
Primo! at Odd Duck was inspired by extra habañero brine
the kitchen was looking to offload to the bar.

El Condor

The drink that keeps you up at night, El Condor's Sonambulo (meaning "sleepwalker") is also the name of an American independent comic book series.

SONAMBULO

El Condor, Los Angeles, California

Makes 1 serving

5   dashes Pernod
1   ounce blanco tequila
¾   ounce Grand Marnier
¾   ounce Cocchi Americano
¾   ounce fresh lime juice
Garnish: expressed orange peel

1. Wash a chilled coupe glass with Pernod*. In a cocktail shaker, add tequila, Grand Marnier, Cocchi Americano, and lime juice. Shake to combine, and strain into prepared glass. Garnish with expressed orange peel, if desired.

*Washing a cocktail glass with Pernod adds the aroma and subtle flavor of the liqueur without overwhelming the palate with the strong taste of anise. To wash, gently swirl the Pernod around the glass to coat, and then discard the excess liquid.

Tequila

BEBIDA DE LOS MUERTOS

The Pinewood, Decatur, Georgia

Makes 1 serving

1-inch square piece of red bell pepper (or another
    spicier pepper)
¾   ounce tequila
¾   ounce Cocchi Americano
¾   ounce Pierre Ferrand Dry Curaçao
¾   ounce fresh lemon juice
2   dashes Bittermens Hopped Grapefruit Bitters

1. Muddle bell pepper in a cocktail shaker. Add ice
and all remaining ingredients, and shake until cold.
Double strain into a coupe glass.

The Pinewood

A play on the classic Corpse Reviver, The Pinewood's beverage director Julian Goglia serves an updated take on the original gin cocktail by using tequila and red bell pepper for a fun and earthy pop of flavor.

Bourbon & Whiskey

BOURBON AND WHISKEY GO BEYOND
"NEAT" WHEN SHAKEN AND SERVED IN A COUPE

Nelson's GreenBrier Distillery

The Vow of Silence is a stirred and spirituous cocktail by the makers of Belle Meade Bourbon, a brand that dates back to the pre-Prohibition era from the Nelson family's American distilling business. The name of this cocktail is derived from the Benedictine Monks who are fabled to take a vow of silence.

THE VOW OF SILENCE

Nelson's Green Brier Distillery, Nashville, Tennessee

Makes 1 serving

2	ounces Belle Meade Bourbon
¾	ounce Carpano Antica Formula
¼	ounce Bénédictine
2	dashes Peychaud's Bitters
1	dash Angostura Bitters

Garnish: expressed lemon peel*

1. Place bourbon, Carpano Antica, Bénédictine, and bitters in a mixing glass, and stir briefly with ice. Strain into a coupe glass. Garnish with expressed lemon peel, if desired.

Using a lighter to heat the lemon peel before "expressing" helps yield more essence/juice. Express by rubbing pith side down between thumb and forefinger.

RISING SUN

Leroy, Montgomery, Alabama

Makes 1 serving

2   ounces Hibiki 12 Year Old Japanese Whisky
1   ounce Lillet Rosé
½   ounce Bang Candy Spiced Smoked Orange
      Simple Syrup
1   dash Miracle Mile Forbidden Bitters
Garnish: orange peel

1. In a cocktail shaker filled with ice, add all
ingredients. Shake to combine, and strain into a
coupe glass. Garnish with an orange peel, if desired.

Leroy

This drink was created with a delicious but slow-moving Japanese whisky and Lillet. The Miracle Mile Forbidden Bitters from Los Angeles works really well with the Bang Candy simple syrup.

Gramercy Tavern

Gramercy Tavern's ode to autumn, the Fall Classic taps into the season's local apple harvest sourced from nearby Union Square Greenmarket. The cocktail is further enhanced with the most classic apple brandy, Calvados, made warmer with locally sourced bourbon.

FALL CLASSIC

Gramercy Tavern, New York, New York

Makes 1 serving

1	ounce bourbon
1	ounce Calvados Apple Brandy
1	ounce fresh apple cider
½	ounce Thyme Simple Syrup (recipe follows)
½	ounce fresh lemon juice
1	dash Angostura Bitters

Garnish: dried or fresh apple slices

1. In a cocktail shaker filled with ice, add bourbon, brandy, cider, Thyme Simple Syrup, lemon juice, and bitters. Shake to combine, and strain into a coupe glass. Garnish with apple slices, if desired.

THYME SIMPLE SYRUP

Makes about ½ cup

½	cup sugar
½	cup water
15	sprigs fresh thyme

1. In small saucepan, bring sugar and ½ cup water to a boil over medium heat, swirling pan to help form syrup. Remove from heat. Add thyme sprigs, and steep until syrup is completely cooled; a clear thyme flavor should come through. Remove and discard thyme. (Syrup should be kept in the refrigerator.)

BARREL-AGED BOULEVARDIER

Sidney Street Cafe, St. Louis, Missouri

Makes 1 serving

1   ounce aged bourbon
1   ounce Campari
1   ounce Martini & Rossi Sweet Vermouth
Garnish: orange twist

1. In a mixing glass filled with ice, add bourbon, Campari, and vermouth. Stir to combine, and strain into a coupe glass. Garnish with an orange twist, if desired.

Sidney Street Cafe

At Sidney Street Cafe, the ingredients of this cocktail are aged together for six months in a Hudson Rye Whiskey barrel before being served from the spigot. If you're not that patient, this adapted recipe using aged bourbon is a great alternative.

Seven Lamps

This off-menu cocktail created
by John Buckhalt is available at
Seven Lamps, Tavernpointe, and
GRAIN in Atlanta.

Longshot

Seven Lamps, Atlanta, Georgia

Makes 1 serving

1½   ounces Angel's Envy
1   ounce Tarragon Syrup (recipe follows)
¾   ounce fresh grapefruit juice
¼   ounce fresh lime juice
Garnish: grapefruit peel

1. In a cocktail shaker filled with ice, add Angel's Envy, Tarragon Syrup, grapefruit juice, and lime juice. Shake to combine, and double strain into a coupe glass. Garnish with a grapefruit peel, if desired.

Tarragon Syrup

Makes about 1 cup

1   cup water
1   cup sugar
¼   cup fresh tarragon

1. In a small saucepan, bring 1 cup water and sugar to a boil over medium-high heat. Reduce heat to medium, and simmer until sugar is dissolved. Stir in tarragon, and remove from heat. Let stand, covered, for 15 minutes. Strain, and let cool.

The Rest

DON'T MISS THESE FABULOUS COCKTAILS
MEANT TO BE SIPPED AND SAVORED

THE COUPE | CHAPTER SEVEN

One Flew South

A play on the classic Jack Rose cocktail,
Tiffanie Barriere's Hoodoo You Love?
at One Flew South was inspired by
Cathead's 66-proof gin-based chicory
liqueur. What's not to love?

HOODOO
YOU LOVE?

One Flew South, Hartsfield-Jackson Atlanta International Airport, Atlanta, Georgia

Makes 1 serving

1½   ounces applejack brandy
½   ounce Cathead Hoodoo Chicory Liqueur
½   ounce fresh lemon juice
½   ounce grenadine
1   large egg white
Garnish: grated cinnamon stick

1. In a cocktail shaker filled with ice, add brandy, chicory liqueur, lemon juice, grenadine, and egg white. Shake to combine, and strain into a coupe glass. Garnish with grated cinnamon stick, if desired.

Eggnog Cocktail

Highlands Bar and Grill, Birmingham, Alabama

Makes 1 serving

2½   ounces Highlands Eggnog (recipe follows)
¾   ounce brandy
¾   ounce Appleton Estate V/X Jamaica Rum
Garnish: fresh grated nutmeg

1. In a cocktail shaker filled with ice, add Highlands Eggnog, brandy, and rum. Shake to combine, and strain into a coupe glass. Garnish with nutmeg, if desired.

Highlands Eggnog

Makes about 7 cups

6   large very fresh farm eggs
1   cup sugar
3   cups whole milk
1   cup heavy whipping cream
Garnish: fresh grated nutmeg

1. Carefully separate egg yolks from whites; refrigerate egg whites.
2. In a medium bowl, whisk together yolks and sugar until smooth. Slowly whisk in milk and cream. Set aside.
3. In another medium bowl, whisk egg whites until two-thirds of mixture is frothy. Skim froth off the top, and stir into yolk mixture. Discard remaining one-third egg whites mixture.
4. Garnish with nutmeg, if desired. Store sealed in a glass jar in the refrigerator for up to 1 day. Shake jar before mixing cocktails.

Highlands Bar and Grill

Each December, the legendary Highlands Bar and Grill serves up the ultimate holiday eggnog experience. Beverage Director Matt Gilpin takes the same care with their homemade eggnog recipe as Chef Frank Stitt does with the exquisite food at Highlands.

West Thirty Six

Muddled sage adds savory notes to this bright
butterscotch cocktail at West Thirty Six.

BUTTERSCOTCH & SAGE SOUR

West Thirty Six, Notting Hill, London, England

Makes 1 serving

5	fresh sage leaves
1½	ounces butterscotch schnapps
¾	ounce Martell Cognac
¾	ounce fresh lemon juice
1	large egg white

Garnish: fresh sage leaves

1. In a cocktail shaker, muddle sage. Add schnapps, cognac, lemon juice, egg white, and ice. Shake to combine, and double strain into a coupe glass. Garnish with sage, if desired.

The Rest

JASON'S ASCENSION, 1988

Cure, New Orleans, Louisiana

Makes 1 serving

1	large egg white
¾	ounce fresh lemon juice
1	ounce pisco
1	ounce La Gitana Manzanilla Sherry
½	ounce grenadine
14	drops Crude Bitterless Marriage Bitters

Garnish: Crude Bitterless Marriage Bitters

1. In a cocktail shaker, add egg white and lemon juice; shake to combine. Add pisco, sherry, grenadine, bitters, and ice, and shake until cold. Double strain into a coupe glass. Garnish with 3 drops bitters, if desired.

Cure

Barman Turk Dietrich of New Orleans's Cure makes a rich, worldly concoction of dry Spanish sherry, Peruvian grape brandy, and floral aromatic bitters from North Carolina. It is elegant without being fussy.

Imperial

Come Out Swinging was Lindsay Baker's first cocktail on the Imperial menu after she assumed bar manager responsibility. The outgoing manager suggested she "come out swinging" with her first menu addition, and so she did with this creative concoction.

COME OUT SWINGING

Imperial, Portland, Oregon

Makes 1 serving

1½   ounces Cachaça
¾   ounce Pommeau
½   ounce Hibiscus Rose Syrup (recipe follows)
½   ounce fresh lime juice
Garnish: lime slice, Luxardo cherry

1. In a cocktail shaker filled with ice, add Cachaça, Pommeau, Hibiscus Rose Syrup, and lime juice. Shake to combine, and double strain into a coupe glass. Garnish with a lime slice and a cherry, if desired.

HIBISCUS ROSE SYRUP

Bring 2 quarts water to a boil. Remove from heat. Add 4 ounces dried hibiscus flowers, and let steep. Let cool completely. Strain out flowers. Add equal amounts of sugar to hibiscus infusion by weight, and cook over low heat until sugar dissolves. Remove from heat. Add one capful of rose water.

Me & Mrs. Jones

Paramour, San Antonio, Texas

Makes 1 serving

1½   ounces VSOP cognac
¾   ounce fresh lemon juice
½   ounce Averna Amaro
⅓   ounce orange marmalade
Fresh rosemary sprig
Garnish: fresh rosemary sprig

1. In a cocktail shaker filled with ice, add cognac, lemon juice, Averna, orange marmalade, and rosemary. Shake to combine, and strain into a coupe glass. Garnish with rosemary, if desired.

Paramour

Paramour's Chris Ware created Me & Mrs. Jones as a playful drink for someone looking for a midday cocktail or affair. The bitterness from Averna Amaro coupled with orange marmalade adds an extra depth of flavor that continues to resonate sip after glorious sip.

Desserts

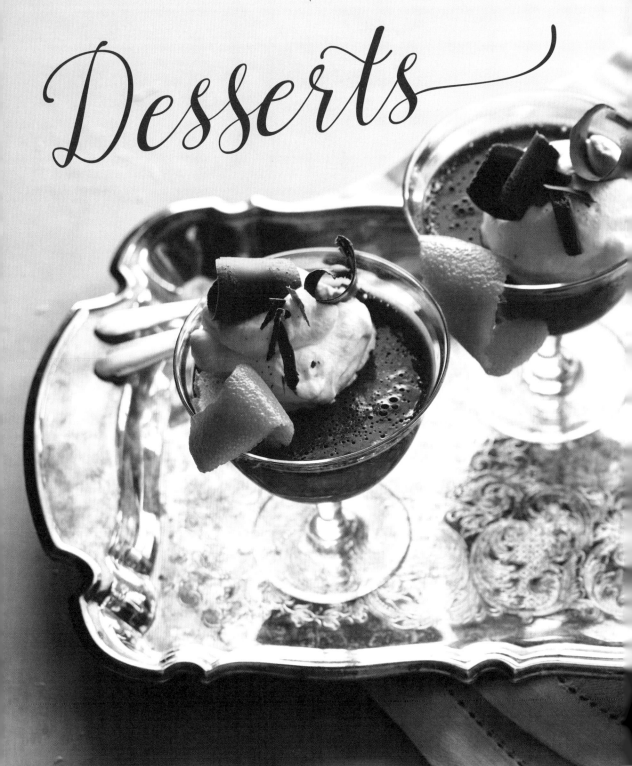

RECIPES FOR EASY
AND ELEGANT
ENTERTAINING

SABAYON
WITH FRESH BERRIES

Makes 6 servings

4   large egg yolks
¼   cup granulated sugar
¼   cup Amaretto
⅔   cup heavy whipping cream
¼   cup confectioners' sugar
½   teaspoon vanilla extract
1   cup quartered fresh strawberries
1   cup fresh raspberries
1   cup fresh blackberries, halved
1   cup fresh blueberries
Garnish: fresh mint

1. Prepare an ice bath large enough to accommodate a medium bowl; set aside.

2. In the top of a double boiler, whisk together egg yolks and granulated sugar. Add Amaretto, and whisk to combine. Continue cooking, whisking constantly, until mixture thickens and appears fluffy and glossy, 10 to 12 minutes. Remove from heat, and set bowl in prepared ice bath. Continue whisking until mixture is completely cooled and thickened.

3. In another medium bowl, beat cream, confectioners' sugar, and vanilla with a mixer at medium-high speed until stiff peaks form. Fold whipped cream into yolk mixture. Serve in coupe glasses with fresh berries. Garnish with mint, if desired. Sabayon can be stored, covered tightly with plastic wrap, in the refrigerator for up to 24 hours.

Inspired by zabaglione, the mousse-like Italian dessert made with eggs, sugar, and white wine, this version substitutes Amaretto for the wine, creating a sweet almond flavor that pairs delightfully with fresh berries.

Double-chocolate brownies layered with caramel filling and topped with chocolate-covered pecans just might be the perfect indulgent dessert.

TURTLE BROWNIES

Makes 8 servings

¾ cup unsalted butter
1 (4-ounce) 60% cacao bittersweet chocolate baking bar, chopped
1¼ cups sugar
2 large eggs
1 cup all-purpose flour
¼ teaspoon baking powder
¼ teaspoon salt
1 cup miniature chocolate morsels
1 teaspoon vanilla extract
Caramel Pie Filling (recipe follows)
Garnish: prepared caramel sauce, Chocolate-Covered Pecans (recipe follows)

1. Preheat oven to 350°. Line bottom and sides of a 9-inch square baking pan with foil, allowing 2 to 3 inches to extend over sides; lightly spray foil with cooking spray.
2. In a large microwave-safe bowl, microwave butter and chopped chocolate on high in 30-second intervals, stirring between each, until melted and smooth (1½ to 2 minutes total). Whisk in sugar. Add eggs, one at a time, whisking until combined after each addition. Whisk in flour, baking powder, and salt. Gently stir in chocolate morsels and vanilla. Pour batter into prepared pan.
3. Bake until a wooden pick inserted in center comes out clean, 18 to 20 minutes. Let cool in pan for 1 hour. Remove from pan, and cut into small triangles.
4. Layer 2 brownie triangles and Caramel Pie Filling in 8 coupe glasses. Repeat layers. Garnish with caramel sauce and Chocolate-Covered Pecans, if desired.

CARAMEL PIE FILLING
Makes 1⅓ cups

1½ cups half-and-half
½ cup firmly packed dark brown sugar
2 large egg yolks
2 tablespoons cornstarch
3 tablespoons butter
1 teaspoon vanilla extract
¼ teaspoon salt

1. In a medium saucepan, combine half-and-half, brown sugar, egg yolks, and cornstarch; whisk until smooth. Cook over medium heat, stirring constantly, until mixture is thick and bubbly. Remove from heat; stir in butter, vanilla, and salt. Transfer to a bowl, and cover with plastic wrap directly on the surface. Refrigerate for at least 2 hours.

CHOCOLATE-COVERED PECANS
Makes 22

½ cup miniature chocolate morsels
1 tablespoon heavy whipping cream
22 pecan halves, toasted

1. In a small microwave-safe bowl, microwave chocolate morsels and cream on high in 30-second intervals, stirring between each, until chocolate is melted and smooth (about 1 minute total). Dip pecans halfway into chocolate, and place on a sheet of parchment paper; let dry.

Lemon Meringue Pies

Makes 4 servings

4   tablespoons lemon zest, divided
1   cup fresh lemon juice
2   (14-ounce) cans sweetened condensed milk
6   large egg yolks
3   tablespoons butter, melted
1   (14.1-ounce) package refrigerated piecrusts
1½   cups sugar, divided
4   large egg whites
1½   teaspoons cream of tartar
Garnish: lemon curls

1. In the top of a double boiler, whisk together 1 tablespoon lemon zest, lemon juice, condensed milk, egg yolks, and melted butter. Cook over simmering water, stirring occasionally, until thickened, about 45 minutes. Remove from heat, and place in a medium bowl. Cover and refrigerate for at least 2 hours.
2. Preheat oven to 400°. Line a baking sheet with parchment paper, and sprinkle with flour.
3. Roll half of dough onto prepared pan. In a small bowl, combine ½ cup sugar and remaining 3 tablespoons lemon zest. Sprinkle over dough. Place remaining dough on top of sugar mixture. Roll from center of dough outward, pressing edges to seal. Cut 8 triangle indentations into dough (do not cut through dough).
4. Bake until light brown and crispy, about 10 minutes. Let cool completely. Cut crust into triangles on indentations.
5. In a medium bowl, beat egg whites and cream of tartar with a mixer at high speed until foamy. Slowly add remaining 1 cup sugar, 1 tablespoon at a time, beating until stiff peaks form.
6. Place half of custard mixture in 4 coupe glasses. Top each with two triangle crusts, and place remaining custard in glasses. Top each with meringue, and brown with a kitchen torch. Garnish with lemon curls, if desired.

This classic pie is
deconstructed with
creamy layers of custard
and meringue elevated by
the zesty flavor of lemon.

The subtle hint of woodsy notes in the rosemary complements the delicate flavor of the pear in this elegant and refreshing treat.

Rosemary Pear Sorbet

Makes 1 quart

1 cup water
1 cup sugar
1 sprig fresh rosemary
½ vanilla bean, split lengthwise, seeds scraped and reserved
4 medium ripe Anjou or Bartlett pears, peeled, cored, and diced
1 cup pear nectar
¼ cup light corn syrup
2 teaspoons fresh lemon juice
½ teaspoon salt
Garnish: Pear Chips (recipe follows)

1. Place a metal loaf pan in the freezer.
2. In a medium saucepan, bring 1 cup water and sugar to a boil over high heat. Reduce heat to medium, and simmer until sugar is dissolved, about 5 minutes. Remove from heat. Add rosemary and reserved vanilla bean seeds. Cover and steep for 25 minutes.
3. Discard rosemary sprigs, and let mixture cool completely, about 1 hour.
4. Refrigerate until cold, about 1 hour.
5. In the container of a blender, combine chilled syrup, pears, pear nectar, corn syrup, lemon juice, and salt; purée until smooth. Cover and refrigerate for at least 1 hour.
6. Pour chilled mixture into an ice cream maker, and freeze according to manufacturer's instructions.
7. Spoon frozen mixture into prepared pan. Cover and freeze until firm, at least 2 hours or overnight. Serve in coupe glasses, and garnish with Pear Chips, if desired. Cover and freeze for up to 1 week.

Pear Chips
Makes about 36

2 cups water, divided
½ cup fresh lemon juice, divided
3 Anjou or Bartlett pears
2 cups sugar
¼ cup light corn syrup

1. In a medium bowl, combine 1 cup water and ¼ cup lemon juice. Using a mandoline, slice pears paper-thin. Place pear slices in lemon water.
2. In a large saucepan, bring sugar, corn syrup, remaining 1 cup water, and remaining ¼ cup lemon juice to a boil over medium-high heat. Reduce heat to medium-low, and cook until sugar is dissolved. Remove from heat, and let cool slightly.
3. Preheat oven to 200°. Line 2 rimmed baking sheets with silicone baking mats.
4. Drain pears, discarding lemon water. Plunge pear slices, a few at a time, into syrup. Let slices stand for 5 to 8 minutes. Remove slices, letting excess syrup drip off. Place slices on prepared pans.
5. Bake until pears are dry to the touch, about 1½ hours. Using an offset spatula, carefully peel pears from pans. Turn pears over; return to oven, and bake until pears are dry and crisp but not browned, about 20 minutes, checking frequently. Let cool completely. Using an offset spatula, carefully remove pear slices. Let dry completely on parchment paper. Store in an airtight container for up to 1 week.

Note: Be sure to choose unripened "green" pears that are firm to the touch. The less ripened the pears are, the more stable they become.

STRAWBERRY CRUNCH

Makes 6 to 8 servings

1½   cups all-purpose flour
⅓   cup granulated sugar
⅓   cup plus 2 tablespoons firmly packed light brown sugar,
      divided
2   tablespoons lemon zest
¼   teaspoon salt
½   cup melted butter
1   (8-ounce) container mascarpone
¼   cup heavy whipping cream
2   cups sliced fresh strawberries
¼   cup Simple Syrup (recipe on page 133)
2   tablespoons chopped fresh mint
Garnish: halved fresh strawberries, fresh mint leaves

1. Preheat oven to 350°. Line a baking sheet with parchment
paper.
2. In a medium bowl, combine flour, granulated sugar,
⅓ cup brown sugar, lemon zest, and salt. Stir in melted butter.
Spread batter on prepared pan.
3. Bake until golden brown, about 10 minutes, stirring twice.
Let cool completely.
4. In a small bowl, combine mascarpone, cream, and remaining
2 tablespoons brown sugar, stirring until smooth. In a medium
bowl, stir together strawberries, Simple Syrup, and mint.
5. Layer strawberries, mascarpone mixture, and crumble in
coupe glasses. Repeat layers. Garnish with strawberries and
mint, if desired.

You'll want seconds of this heavenly dessert, made with fresh strawberries, creamy mascarpone, and crispy crumble.

Smothered with a pile of crunchy Glazed Mixed Nuts, this sweet and salty treat packs a punch with the flavor of traditional Scotch whisky.

Salted Butterscotch Pudding with Glazed Mixed Nuts

Makes 4 servings

¾   cup firmly packed dark brown sugar
¼   cup firmly packed light brown sugar
2   tablespoons cornstarch
1½   cups half-and-half
½   cup heavy whipping cream
1½   tablespoons Scotch whisky
2   tablespoons butter, softened
1   teaspoon vanilla extract
⅛   teaspoon fleur de sel
Glazed Mixed Nuts (recipe follows)
Garnish: fleur de sel

1. In a medium saucepan, whisk together brown sugars and cornstarch. Add half-and-half, cream, and Scotch. Cook over medium-high heat, whisking often. Bring mixture to a boil, and boil for 1 minute. Remove from heat. Add butter, vanilla, and salt. Transfer to a container, and let cool for 20 minutes. Cover with plastic wrap, pressing directly on surface, and refrigerate for 2 hours.
2. Divide pudding among coupe glasses. Serve with Glazed Mixed Nuts. Garnish with fleur de sel, if desired. Cover and refrigerate for up to 3 days.

Glazed Mixed Nuts
Makes 2 cups

1   (15-ounce) can mixed nuts
3   tablespoons Salted Butterscotch Sauce (recipe follows)

1. In a small bowl, combine nuts and Salted Butterscotch Sauce, stirring to coat well. Use immediately.

Salted Butterscotch Sauce
Makes about 1½ cups

¼   cup butter
1   cup firmly packed light brown sugar
½   cup granulated sugar
¼   teaspoon cream of tartar
¼   cup half-and-half
¼   cup dark corn syrup
1   tablespoon Scotch whisky
1   teaspoon vanilla extract
1   pinch fleur de sel

1. In a medium saucepan, melt butter over medium-high heat. Add brown sugar, granulated sugar, cream of tartar, half-and-half, and corn syrup; bring mixture to a boil. Reduce heat to medium, and cook for 5 minutes, stirring frequently. Add Scotch, vanilla, and salt, whisking to combine. Remove from heat, and let cool to room temperature. Extra sauce can be stored, covered with plastic wrap touching surface, at room temperature for up to 5 days.

CHOCOLATE-ORANGE POTS DE CRÈME

Makes 6 servings

2   cups half-and-half
10   ounces 60% cacao bittersweet chocolate, chopped
2   teaspoons orange zest
2   tablespoons orange liqueur
2   large egg yolks
Garnish: sweetened whipped cream, orange curls, chocolate curls

1. In a medium saucepan, bring half-and-half to a boil over medium-high heat.
2. Place chocolate, orange zest, and orange liqueur in the container of a blender. Carefully pour in hot half-and-half, and let stand for 1 minute. Blend until smooth. With blender running, add egg yolks, one at a time. Let mixture cool slightly.
3. Divide mixture among 6 coupe glasses, and cover with plastic wrap. Refrigerate until firm, 2 to 4 hours or overnight. Garnish with whipped cream, orange curls, and chocolate curls, if desired.

Rich chocolate pairs beautifully with
the fresh citrus flavor of orange,
taking these traditional French
dessert custards to the next level.

Citrus is the highlight of this creamy mousse, which is enhanced by tangy Candied Orange Slices and beautiful Caramelized Hazelnuts.

Grand Marnier Mousse with Candied Orange Slices and Caramelized Hazelnuts

Makes 6 servings

¾ cup heavy whipping cream
1   cup confectioners' sugar, divided
2   teaspoons orange zest, divided
1   (8-ounce) package cream cheese, softened
1   (8-ounce) container crème fraîche, softened
3   tablespoons Grand Marnier
½   teaspoon vanilla extract
Candied Orange Slices (recipe follows)
Caramelized Hazelnuts (recipe follows)

1. In a medium bowl, beat cream, ¼ cup confectioners' sugar, and 1 teaspoon orange zest with a mixer at medium-high speed until stiff peaks form. Cover and refrigerate until chilled.
2. In another medium bowl, beat cream cheese with a mixer at medium-high speed until smooth, about 3 minutes. Add crème fraîche, and beat until combined, about 2 minutes. Add Grand Marnier, vanilla, remaining ¾ cup confectioners' sugar, and remaining 1 teaspoon orange zest, beating to combine. Fold whipped cream mixture into cream cheese mixture. Spoon into coupe glasses. Cover and refrigerate for at least 1 hour or up to 3 days. Serve with Candied Orange Slices and Caramelized Hazelnuts.

Candied Orange Slices
Makes about 36

3   cups water
1   cup sugar
3 to 4 oranges*, sliced ⅛ to ¼ inch thick, seeds removed

1. Spray a large piece of parchment paper with cooking spray.
2. In a large heavy-bottomed skillet, bring 3 cups water and sugar to a boil over high heat. Add orange slices in a shingle fashion. Reduce heat to medium, and simmer for 8 to 10 minutes, turning orange slices once or twice.
3. Reduce heat to medium-low, and continue simmering for about 20 minutes, turning orange slices occasionally. Remove from heat, and let cool. Let oranges stand in liquid for 10 to 12 minutes.
4. Using tongs, carefully remove slices, and set out to dry on prepared parchment paper. Store, covered, between layers of parchment paper at room temperature for up to 3 days.

Any type of orange can be used. We used a combination of Moro, Cara Cara, navel oranges, and kumquats.

Caramelized Hazelnuts
Makes about 1½ cups

12 hazelnuts, toasted and peeled
12 (12-inch) wooden skewers
1   cup sugar
¼   cup water

1. Line a rimmed baking sheet with parchment paper. Place a heavy cutting board at the edge of countertop; place prepared pan onto floor directly below cutting board.
2. Thread one hazelnut onto the end of each wooden skewer, pressing gently and twisting to secure; set aside.
3. In a small heavy saucepan, cook sugar and ¼ cup water over medium-high heat. Cook, stirring occasionally, until sugar is dissolved. Continue to cook, without stirring, until syrup comes to a boil. Using a wet pastry brush, carefully wash down sides of pan to prevent crystals from forming. Continue to cook until sugar registers 340° on a candy thermometer and is a deep amber color. Remove from heat, and let cool for 8 to 10 minutes.
4. Working quickly, dip skewered hazelnuts into caramel, one at a time, rolling to coat completely. Let excess drip back into pan. Secure end of skewers beneath cutting board, and let excess caramel drip onto prepared pan. Let hazelnuts stand until caramel is hardened, 6 to 8 minutes. Using kitchen shears, cut caramel strings to desired length. Carefully remove hazelnuts from skewers. Use immediately.

Banana Pudding

Makes 6 servings

2	cups whole milk
1	cup sugar, divided
⅓	cup all-purpose flour
¼	teaspoon salt
4	large egg yolks
1	cup white chocolate morsels
1	teaspoon vanilla extract
3	large bananas, sliced and divided
12	shortbread cookies*
¼	cup Baileys Irish Cream
1	cup sweetened whipped cream

White chocolate curls

1. In a medium saucepan, combine milk, ¾ cup sugar, flour, salt, and egg yolks, whisking until smooth. Cook over medium heat, whisking constantly, until thickened and bubbly. Remove from heat; stir in white chocolate morsels and vanilla until melted. Let cool for 30 minutes.

2. Heat a medium skillet over medium-high heat. Dip 12 banana slices in remaining ¼ cup sugar. Place slices in hot skillet, and cook until golden, about 1 minute per side. Set aside.

3. Dip cookies in Baileys to coat. Layer pudding, cookies, and remaining banana slices in 6 coupe glasses. Top each with whipped cream, 2 caramelized banana slices, and white chocolate curls.

We used Lorna Doone Shortbread Cookies.

With layers of pudding, cream, and caramelized bananas, this decadent dessert is made better by the hint of Baileys Irish Cream coating crunchy shortbread cookies.

Twist & Twirl

FROM SEXY SHARDS OF
ORANGE PEEL TO SPIRALING
LEMON TWISTS, CITRUS
GARNISHES ARE OFTEN THE
FINISHING TOUCH ON MANY
COCKTAILS. NOT ONLY DOES
THE COLOR OF CITRUS
ADD VISUAL IMPACT, BUT
ITS FRAGRANT OILS
ENHANCE THE FLAVOR
OF MANY CRAFT
COCKTAILS.

Tips for Making Beautiful Citrus Garnishes

- Use a Y-shaped peeler for wide pieces of peel
- A channel knife creates long spirals. Wrap them around your finger for a few seconds to help them keep their shape.
- Remove as little white pith as possible
- Choose ripe, unblemished citrus and leave it at room temperature
- Using a lighter to heat citrus peel before "expressing" helps yield more essence/juice. Express by rubbing pith side down between thumb and forefinger

SIMPLE *Syrups*

THIS QUICK MIXTURE OF SUGAR AND WATER CAN BE EASILY INFUSED WITH A VARIETY OF INGREDIENTS TO ADD FLAVOR DEPTH TO YOUR COUPE COCKTAILS

SPICE SYRUP

PEPPER SYRUP

SIMPLE SYRUP

Simple syrups can be covered and refrigerated for up to 3 weeks.

To make these flavor variations, prepare basic Simple Syrup first.

SIMPLE SYRUP

In a small saucepan, bring 2 cups water and 2 cups sugar to a boil over medium-high heat. Reduce heat to medium, and simmer until sugar is dissolved. Remove from heat, and let cool completely.

SPICE SYRUP

Add 12 pink or black peppercorns, 6 whole cloves, 4 whole allspice, 2 green cardamom pods, 2 cinnamon sticks, and 2 star anise to sugar mixture once removed from heat. Let steep for 20 minutes. Strain mixture, and let cool completely.

PEPPER SYRUP

Add 2 sliced jalapeño peppers and 2 sliced serrano peppers to sugar mixture once removed from heat. Let steep for 20 minutes. Strain mixture, and let cool completely.

VANILLA SYRUP

Add 2 vanilla beans with their scraped seeds and 2 teaspoons vanilla extract to sugar mixture once removed from heat. Let steep for 20 minutes. Strain mixture, and let cool completely.

CITRUS SYRUP

Add 1 sliced lemon, 1 peeled lemon, 1 sliced small orange, 1 small peeled orange, and 3 sliced kumquats to sugar mixture once removed from heat. Let steep for 20 minutes. Strain mixture, and let cool completely.

HERB SYRUP

Add 4 sprigs fresh rosemary or other herb to sugar mixture once removed from heat. Let steep for 20 minutes. Strain mixture, and let cool completely.

ACKNOWLEDGEMENTS

To my mom, Phyllis Hoffman DePiano, who's joined me in my coupe quest to make sure my bar cart always showcases a unique collection for any occasion

To Brooke Bell, Deanna Gardner, and Mary Beth Jones, my creative team that joined me with mutual passion to execute my vision on every page. You brought the hashtags #coupelife and #coupin to life.

To my coworkers at Hoffman Media for your creative abilities and dedication to this dream project

To Stephen DeVries for capturing the vision of my mind's eye

To Patrick Dunne for your eloquent words, incredible culinary knowledge, and always-impressive selection of antique French coupes

To Matt Gilpin for helping me declare the "year of the coupe" and for always entertaining my earlier every year request for your eggnog. Do you think October is too early this year?

To our photography location partners, Pardis and Frank Stitt, for your warm hospitality and dedicated use of the coupe in your restaurants. Your relationship is invaluable to me.

To all of the barkeeps and mixologists that shared recipes with us, thank you for serving your craft cocktails in coupes every night

To my husband Stephen Hart Hoffman for allowing our cabinets to be full of coupes. Your question of "Do we really need more of these?" will always be answered with an excited, "We do!"

Santé!

INDEX

RESOURCES & NOTES

Page 2: Cocktail napkins by Sferra, Linen Way, and Henry Handwork; custom monogramming by Bobbins Design

Page 6: Camille Champagne coupe glass available at Crate and Barrel

Page 7: Coupe cocktail glasses available at Williams-Sonoma

Page 13: Camille Champagne coupe glass available at Crate and Barrel

Pages 14-15: Diamond-cut mixing glass available at Sur La Table; Soho Cocktail Shaker available at Wayfair; cocktail strainer available at World Market

Page 16: Antique bar cart from Huff Harrington Home

Page 17: Gold-rimmed coupe glasses from Sur La Table; antique Champagne bucket from Dovetail Antiques

Page 20: Camille Champagne coupe glass available at Crate and Barrel

Page 24: Jasper cocktail glass available at Crate and Barrel

Page 27: Elegance By Lenox in Champagne/Tall Sherbet available at Replacements

Page 28: Coupe cocktail glasses available at Williams-Sonoma; copper cocktail shaker available at Pottery Barn

Page 31: Camille Champagne coupe glass available at Crate and Barrel

Page 35: Coupe glasses available at Table Matters; Linen Way cocktail napkins with custom monogramming available at Bobbins Design

Page 36: Monroe coupe glass with gold trim by Lenox available at Replacements; cocktail shaker available at Pottery Barn

Page 40: Camille Champagne coupe glass available at Crate and Barrel

Page 43: Fusion Champagne Coupe Glass available at Wayfair

Page 45: Cocktail napkin by Sferra

Page 52: Massena by Baccarat Champagne/Tall Sherbet available at Replacements

Page 59: Hartland Coupe by Simon Pearce

Page 62: Vintage coupe glasses from The St. George's Foundation Second-Hand Rose Charity Shoppe

Page 66: Gold-encrusted Massenet Champagne/Tall Sherbet by St Louis available at Replacements

Page 69: Linen Way cocktail napkins with custom monogramming available at Bobbins Design

Page 76: Allure By Lenox in Champagne/Tall Sherbet available at Replacements

Page 79: Vintage coupe glasses from The St. George's Foundation Second-Hand Rose Charity Shoppe

Page 80: Gold-rimmed coupe glass from Sur La Table

Page 85: Cocktail shaker available at Pier 1; muddler available at Sur La Table; cocktail napkin by Sferra

Page 86: Gold Trim Intrigue by Lenox in Champagne/Tall Sherbet available at Replacements

Page 94: Schott Zwiesel® Bar Collection Champagne coupe glasses available at Sur La Table

Page 97: Mixing glass available at Wayfair

Page 109: Dorset Champagne Coupe glasses available at Williams-Sonoma

Page 113: Queen by Rogaska in Champagne/Tall Sherbet available at Replacements

Page 117: Dorset Champagne Coupe glasses available at Williams-Sonoma

Page 118: Vintage coupe glasses from The St. George's Foundation Second-Hand Rose Charity Shoppe

Page 121: Hartland Coupe by Simon Pearce

Page 122: Versailles-Blue by Fostoria in Champagne/Tall Sherbet available at Replacements; cocktail napkin by Sferra

Page 126: (Front glass) Allure by Lenox in Champagne/Tall Sherbet available at Replacements; (middle glass) Camille Champagne coupe available at Crate and Barrel; (back glass) Jasper cocktail glass available at Crate and Barrel

Surfaces by Erickson Wood Works: *ericksonwoodworks.com*

Bobbins Design: *bobbinsdesign.com*

Crate and Barrel: *crateandbarrel.com*

Dovetail Antiques: 828-743-1800

Henry Handwork: *henryhandwork.com*

Huff Harrington Home: *huffharrington.com*

Linen Way: *linenway.com*

Pier 1: *pier1.com*

Pottery Barn: *potterybarn.com*

Replacements: *replacements.com*

Sferra: *sferra.com*

Simon Pearce: *simonpearce.com*

Sur La Table: *surlatable.com*

Table Matters: *table-matters.com*

The St. George's Foundation Second-Hand Rose Charity Shoppe: *stgeorgesfoundation .org/about/world-heritage-centre/merchandise/*

Wayfair: *wayfair.com*

Williams-Sonoma: *williams-sonoma.com*

World Market: *worldmarket.com*

A note regarding the use of raw eggs:

Egg whites are a classic cocktail element. When shaken, eggs give cocktails a fizzy, frothy texture. Always use the freshest, highest quality eggs available. Those with compromised immune systems and the elderly should not consume raw eggs. Pasteurized eggs can be substituted.

Photography Credits

Page 22: Photo courtesy Masseria

Page 25: Photo courtesy Birds & Bubbles

Page 26: Photo courtesy Burlock Coast

Page 30: Photo courtesy Brennan's Restaurant

Page 34: Photo courtesy Joseph Woodley

Page 38: Photo courtesy Green Olive Media

Page 46: Photo courtesy Marcel's

Page 49: Photo courtesy Edmund's Oast

Page 53: Photo courtesy Green Olive Media

Page 54: Photo courtesy PassionFish

Page 57: Photo courtesy Russell House Tavern

Page 58: Photo courtesy Adrienne Dever

Page 64: Photo courtesy Andrea Calo

Page 68: Photo courtesy Brennan's Restaurant

Page 71: Photo courtesy Aviary

Page 74: Photo courtesy Brett Hufziger

Page 77: Photo courtesy Porchlight

Page 82: Photo courtesy Justen Clay

Page 87: Photo courtesy Nelson's Green Brier Distillery

Page 91: Photo courtesy Gramercy Tavern

Page 92: Photo courtesy Sidney Street Cafe

Page 95: Photo courtesy Green Olive Media

Page 103: Photo courtesy West Thirty Six

Page 107: Photo courtesy Imperial